Eastman Johnson's

Lake Superior Indians

Eastman Johnson's

Lake Superior Indians

Text by Patricia Condon Johnston

Johnston Publishing Inc.   Afton, Minnesota

Also by Patricia Condon Johnston
Stillwater
Minnesota's Birthplace
in photographs by John Runk
Address inquiries to:
Johnston Publishing Inc.
Box 96
Afton, MN 55001

A portion of *Eastman Johnson's Lake Superior Indians*
first appeared in *American History Illustrated*
(February, 1983) in different form.

for Charlie

Introduction

The most important collection owned by the St. Louis County Historical Society is a group of oil paintings and charcoal drawings depicting Ojibwe Indian life at Grand Portage and what is now Duluth-Superior. Created by noted American artist Eastman Johnson, this collection of thirty-six works provides unique insight into the character of Ojibwe life at the midpoint of the nineteenth century. They are among the earliest visual records of the western Lake Superior region that exist, and they are also among the very few examples of the Ojibwe Indian in American art.

Acquired and saved through the generosity of one man, Richard Teller Crane, the St. Louis Historical Society has been the owner and guardian of this collection since the 1920s. Now on permanent display at the Society's Depot Museum, these Eastman Johnson paintings and drawings are viewed by nearly a quarter-million people each year.

The Society is pleased to cooperate with Patricia Condon Johnston in the publication of this book and hopes it will provide an even better understanding and appreciation of Eastman Johnson's legacy to Minnesota.

Lawrence J. Sommer, Director

St. Louis County Historical Society
Duluth, Minnesota

January, 1983

Illustrations

Illustrations

Eastman Johnson's

Lake Superior Indians

Log Cabin Interior — Pokegama Bay.
Charcoal and crayon on paper, 8¼x10¼ inches.
This drawing is thought to be a self-portrait of Johnson in the
cabin he built for himself during his first visit to Lake Superior.

Eastman Johnson was the most celebrated American genre painter of his era. Lionized during the 1860s and 1870s for his sensitive paintings of country life, his subjects were commonly haymakers and cornhuskers, cranberry pickers and maple sugar makers. Less well-known is a series of paintings and drawings made earlier in his career of the native Ojibwe at Lake Superior. Curiously, he never chose to exhibit these pictures. The collection nonetheless ranks with the finest examples of Indians in art in the nineteenth century.

Just back from Europe after completing several years of art training in Germany, Holland, and France, and before establishing himself in the East, Johnson visited his sister Sarah and her husband, William Newton, in Superior, Wisconsin, during the summer of 1856. As general manager for the land company at the head of the lakes, Newton had staked a claim on the townsite of Superior and was one of its proprietors. Johnson's brother Reuben was also operating a sawmill in Superior. Indian title to the north shore land had been extinguished two years before in 1854, the same year that Superior was surveyed and platted, and the town was booming.

Johnson had several reasons for coming to Superior. He was renewing family ties on the one hand, but he was also anxious to speculate in local real estate. Besides his own capital, his father had given him $500 to invest. At a time when American Indians were thought to be a vanishing species, the Ojibwe who still lived in large numbers in the area were yet another attraction. Johnson had already decided to paint American themes, but he was still searching for suitable subject matter.

While he stayed at the Newton house, the largest in town and a favorite gathering place, Johnson seems to have been an enthusiastic participant in the family's busy social life. Reportedly, he was "as frolicksome as anybody" at a Christmas party in 1856, and on another occasion he enlivened an evening by making portrait sketches of the guests inside the roses on the Newton wallpaper. Johnson painted at least a couple of portraits of settlers' wives, one of them his sister, in Superior in 1856, but more of his time was spent savoring the primitive beauty of his new-found environment.

Landscape of Superior, Wisconsin.
Charcoal and crayon on paper, 16¾x22½ inches.
Rich in historical content, this view of Superior was sketched
from George Stuntz's trading post on Minnesota Point in 1857.
The town's first hotel, the Nicollet House, is seen in the
background, and the large building emitting the smoke is the
sawmill at the lumber yard at Detroit Pier which was run by
Johnson's brother, Reuben. The steamer on the left is the
Lady Elgin which foundered with three hundred persons
on board in 1860.

Cutting himself off temporarily from civilization, Johnson built a cabin of cedar logs on Pokegama Bay (on the bank of the St. Louis River opposite the present location of Duluth), and hired Stephen Bonga, a mixed-blood of Indian and black descent, as his guide and interpreter. Together the two traveled Lake Superior's shore, exploring the Apostle Islands, and journeying as far as Isle Royale in Michigan. Bonga called Johnson a "most likeable man to work for," and said that his employer became an expert at handling a birchbark canoe. Years later, local historian John Bardon, who was born in Superior in 1863, used Johnson's cabin for boyhood hunting trips. Bonga had identified it for him as Johnson's, Bardon said, adding that it "had a Southern Style, broad fire-place and a wing chair, crane and bake oven."

Once the ice was out in the spring, Johnson went back to Washington, D.C. It had been a year and a half since he had returned from Europe, and it was time he got on with earning a livelihood. George Washington's deteriorating mansion at Mount Vernon provided a picturesque subject for his brush, but the view he painted of it was undistinguished. (Johnson simply was never at his best at landscapes.) That same summer, frustrated perhaps, and apparently unready to dismiss the call of the wilderness, the artist returned to Superior. Most of Johnson's superb paintings and drawings of the Lake Superior Ojibwe are the result of this second trip west in 1857.

Including a self-portrait of Johnson in his log cabin lair, there are thirty-five pictures in the Duluth collection: thirteen oil paintings, one colored pastel, and twenty-one charcoal sketches. Two of the sketches have only recently been discovered. They were found on the backs of other drawings when the collection was being restored in 1978. Except for one oil, *Oweenie of the Chippewas,* which the St. Louis County Historical Society purchased from a western art dealer in 1983, the entire collection was presented to the city of Duluth by Chicago businessman Richard Teller Crane in 1908. (The historical society also owns an oil portrait by Johnson of his brother-in-law, William Newton, which was donated by Newton family relatives in 1968, and is displayed with the Indian collection.)

Camp Scene at Grand Portage.
Oil on canvas, 4¾x13 inches.
The Ojibwe settlement at Grand Portage. Eastman Johnson's
paintings and drawings are the earliest known illustrations of
this historic Minnesota site.

Biographer John I.H. Baur feels that Johnson might have been influenced in his decision to paint Indians by the novels of James Fenimore Cooper. This is a possibility, but he was also following the lead of several American artists including George Catlin, James Otto Lewis, Seth Eastman, and Henry Lewis, all of whom produced pictorial records of Indian life in the Northwest. It is likely that Johnson even knew Henry Lewis when both were members of the American art colony in Düsseldorf in 1851.

There was also what amounted to an artistic mission afoot in this country to correct the centuries-old stock images of American Indians. Johnson surely was familiar with his friend Henry Wadsworth Longfellow's epic poem, *Hiawatha.* (Published in 1855, *Hiawatha* was based on Henry Rowe Schoolcraft's research among the Ojibwe.) In 1856 *The Crayon,* a well-read art periodical, took up the cause in its January issue in an editorial, "The Indians in American Art":

Grand Portage.
Oil on canvas, 9x19½ inches.
The view is looking east from the site of the old
North West Company post toward Mount Josephine.

It seems to us that the Indian has not received justice in American art.... It should be held in dutiful remembrance that he is fast passing away from the face of the earth. Soon the last red man will have faded forever from his native land, and those who come after us will trust to our scanty records for their knowledge of his habits and appearance.... Absorbed in his quiet dignity, brave, honest, eminently truthful, and always thoroughly in earnest, he stands grandly apart from all other known savage life. As such, let him be, for justice sake, sometimes represented.

Working chiefly at Pokegama Bay and at Grand Portage, 150 miles from Superior on the north shore of Lake Superior at the Canadian border, Johnson made both individual portraits and group scenes of the Ojibwe. The Indians are seen sitting, walking, riding in a canoe, and standing beside their tepees. There are also landscapes depicting Grand Portage, an important early fur trading center, which show the Indians in camp, and one of Superior's harbor in 1857.

From a practical standpoint, the collection is a valuable record of Lake Superior's Ojibwe at the beginning of a transitory period in their history. Placed in the context of American art, it becomes something infinitely more. These are not merely candid images. Instead, they bespeak Johnson's enormous talent for portraiture. Coming at the onset of his career, the Indian portfolio confirms the artistic prowess that enabled him to climb quickly to the top of his profession.

Studies of Ojibwe Woman and Child.
(Ma dos way beek)
Charcoal and crayon on paper, 10x5¼ inches.
The name means "Ten Dollars".

Wigemar Wasung.
Charcoal and crayon on paper, 10¼x8 inches.

Jonathan Eastman Johnson (he soon dropped the Jonathan) was born in Lovell, Maine, on July 29, 1824, the third of eight children of Philip Carrigan and Mary Chandler Johnson. While he was still a toddler, the family moved to nearby Fryeburg, Maine, and later to Augusta, the state capital, where Philip held various government positions including Secretary of State. Eastman's brother, Philip Johnson, Jr., later a rear admiral in the United States Navy, recalled that "when the family drove into the little town of Augusta...I can remember quite distinctly riding with my brothers Reuben and Eastman standing on a board fastened on the outside, back of the sleigh.... 'Twas a very cold day when we arrived at a little wooden cottage on Pleasant Street." (Decades later the artist returned to the scene of his childhood to paint some of his most important genre paintings, and for five years in the early 1860s he spent three months each spring in the maple groves at Fryeburg.)

By the time he was about fifteen, young Eastman had finished his formal schooling. He left Augusta in 1839 and went to Concord, New Hampshire, to clerk in a dry goods store, but it quickly became evident that he had little interest in commerce. This was followed by a stint in a lithography shop in Boston where his father sent him to learn the trade, and he designed titles for books and music. In 1842, at the age of eighteen, Eastman was back in Augusta, doing what he did best — crayon portraits of his family, friends, and neighbors. He converted a room in the house to a studio, hung out a shingle that said he was accepting commissions, and surprisingly enough, he got them.

Sha Wen ne gun.
Charcoal and crayon on paper, 7¼x7½ inches.
The name means "Southern Feather," or, less likely,
"Southern Bone."

Johnson made a modest living during the next few years as something of an itinerant limner, traveling from town to town. His early portraits appear to be good likenesses, and in an era before the camera, this would have been the most important consideration to his Yankee patrons. Late in 1844 or early the next year, he established a studio in Washington, D.C., where the number of possible clients was greater, and where he hoped to assemble a portfolio of drawings of prominent Americans. (His father was expecting an appointment with the Department of the Navy and followed his son to the capital in 1846.) Perhaps due to his father's influence, a senate committee room was set aside for the young artist. Those who sat for him included judges of the Supreme Court, John Quincy Adams, Daniel Webster, and Mrs. Alexander Hamilton.

On March 16, 1846, Johnson wrote to his father that he was also doing a portrait of Dolley Madison, then in her eighties. (When the British set fire to Washington in 1814, it was Mrs. Madison who had the presence of mind to rescue Gilbert Stuart's portrait of George Washington before fleeing the burning President's House.) "She comes in at 10 o'clock in full dress for the occasion," said Johnson, "and as she has much taste in this matter, she looks quite imposing with her white satin turban and black velvet dress and a countenance so full of benignity and gentleness. She talks a great deal and in such quick, beautiful tones. So polished and elegant are her manners that it is a pleasure to be in her company. I think I shall make a fine portrait." Mrs. Madison's portrait was indeed "fine," and Johnson used it as an advertisement to secure additional commissions. Later, refusing to part with the original, he copied the drawing for Daniel Webster.

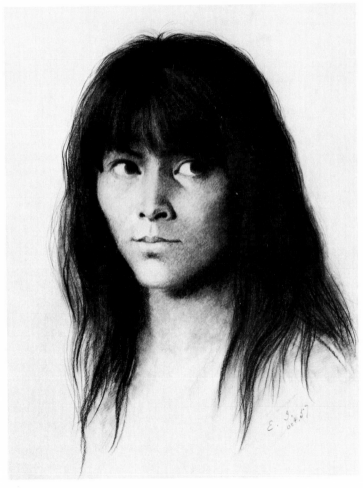

Ojibwe Head.
Charcoal and crayon on paper, 16¾x13¼ inches.

Henry Wadsworth Longfellow was another of Johnson's admirers. In 1846 the poet lured him to Boston to draw portraits of himself and his family. Johnson had studios in Amory Hall and later in Tremont Temple in the city, and Longfellow gives some indication of the artist's method of working in these entries from his journal:

September 17: "Went to town.... To Johnson's room, who made an outline of my face."

September 19: "In Town. Young Johnson began a crayon sketch of my head. From the first sitting I augur well of it."

October 1: "Went to town and gave Johnson a sitting."

October 6: "Went to Johnson's room. All delighted with his portrait of me, thinking it the best ever made."

Longfellow also ordered portraits of several of his friends including Charles Sumner, Nathaniel Hawthorne, and Ralph Waldo Emerson. Johnson delighted in working with these members of the Cambridge literary colony and was especially fond of Emerson. "No one ever impressed me so as being a perfectly spiritual man, in mind, in appearance, and manner," he said. "His aspect was gentle and lovely; his talk like an angel. He was a perfect saint — better

than that." Emerson's ideas concerning American art and literature also undoubtedly appealed to Johnson.

"We have listened too long to the courtly muses of Europe," Emerson warned. He urged poets and artists to consider local subjects: "We have yet had no genius in America with tyrannous eye, which knew the value of our incomparable material.... Our logrolling, our stumps, and their politics, our fisheries, our Negros and Indians, our boats...the northern trade, the southern planting, the western clearing, Oregon and Texas, are yet unsung. Yet America is a poem in our eyes; its ample geography dazzles the imagination."

Johnson remained in Boston for three years and formed close friendships with artists George Henry Hall and Samuel Rowse. Like Johnson, Rowse was doing pencil and crayon portraits for which he charged twenty-five dollars. Presumably, Johnson's fees were similar. Hall later remembered that Johnson was working confidently and rapidly by now, seldom needing to make corrections. Two or three sittings at most were enough for a portrait, and his drawings were often finished in a single day. But Johnson himself was keenly aware of his own limitations.

Ojibwe Woman.
Charcoal and crayon on paper, 6¼x5½ inches.

Study of Ojibwe Woman.
Charcoal and crayon on paper, 8¼x7¾ inches.

America was without proper art schools, and his only training had been in high school. Johnson experimented with pastels in Boston and possibly attempted painting in oils, but he was still using crayons for his portraits. The solution was to go abroad where he could receive instruction and study the old masters firsthand.

On July 15, 1849, with George Hall, Johnson sailed for Europe on the *William Shakespeare* (one of the Dramatic line of ships which featured a full-length wood carving of the bard on its bow). Relying on the advice of Andrew Warner, the secretary of the American Art-Union, a non-profit organization whose stated aims were "cultivating the talents of artists" and "promoting the popular taste," the two had booked passage for Düsseldorf. "It is thought that better opportunities for a student in painting are offered in Germany than in Italy at this time," Warner told them. The German city was a world art center, specifically known for its superior genre painters whose style was rapidly catching on with American collectors.

A search of archival records has failed to turn up Johnson's name among those who were formally enrolled at the Royal Academy, but a large sketchbook at the Brooklyn Museum inscribed "E. Johnson/Royal Academy of Düsseldorf/Anatomical Class/1849" indicates his participation in at least one class at the school. It is likely that he was also admitted to painting classes. In October, 1850, he shipped two paintings to the American Art-Union for sale. These pieces, *Peasants of the Rhine* and *The Junior Partner* have disappeared, but several drawings from this period show a definite technical improvement in Johnson's portrait work. His approach to his subjects is more aesthetic; he is no longer content to simply record their facial features. Where he once used light and shadow to emphasize individual characteristics, these elements now serve to unify the form. His touch is lighter and the images more artful.

Unfinished Sketch of Ojibwe Woman.
Charcoal and crayon on paper, 10½x9 inches.

In Düsseldorf, Johnson also came under the influence of Emanuel Leutze, a giant among American painters and president of the Kneiper Club, an artists' fraternity which welcomed Johnson as a member. Leutze had recently rented an immense atelier where he was completing his masterpiece, *Washington Crossing the Delaware.* (Now at the Metropolitan Museum of Art, this canvas measures more than twenty-one feet long and twelve feet high; its figures are life-size.) Johnson joined Leutze for riding lessons at a local military academy and began painting in his studio in January, 1851. Several artists besides Leutze worked under his direction on the Washington painting, but Johnson was not one of them. For his part, Johnson secured a replica of George Washington's uniform made by a tailor from his father in Washington. With Leutze's assistance, he also made a smaller copy of the famous painting for a French publisher.

The mood was congenial at Leutze's and the artistic atmosphere stimulating, wrote Johnson in a letter to Andrew Warner at the Art-Union. "I regret now that I had not been with him during my entire stay in Düsseldorf." In another letter to a neighbor girl back home in Augusta, he elaborates on the working conditions at Leutze's:

With six in a room, a cask of the best...beer always behind the canvas and a disposition to be jolly you may be sure it does not want for animation. Leutze is an energetic talkative fellow, generous and full of spirits.... To give a more decided tone to the place three cannons were recently brot [sic] and a battery constructed with the stars and stripes waving on one side and the black and white of Prussia on the other. Nothing could exceed the enjoyment produced by the sound of the entire battery, so that almost every one that enters is received with three guns, and accordingly up to the present time there has been a pretty uninterrupted cannonade. The fun has been increased by shooting with bullets also, and the walls are fearfully scarred with the continued bombardment.

29

Despite the six months or so he spent with Leutze, however, Johnson was disappointed with his progress at the end of two years in Düsseldorf. Except for Leutze, he said, he found the current artists in the city poor colorists, judging them "scarcely tolerable." He toured Holland and London in the summer of 1851, then cut his Düsseldorf ties and moved to The Hague. The next three and a half years were spent immersing himself in the work of the Dutch masters.

Rembrandt was a particular favorite of his, and Johnson made so many copies of his paintings that friends dubbed him the "American Rembrandt." With the help of the American ambassador to The Hague, August Belmont, he also secured numerous portrait commissions. (One of these is a picture of Belmont's son, Perry, at the age of two and a half, dressed in a sailor suit and waving an American flag.) These portraits and several complex genre paintings made in Holland reveal Johnson's indebtedness to Rembrandt and his contemporaries. He had mastered oil portraiture and become adept at coloring and composition.

By all accounts, the rising young artist fared well in the Dutch capital. He mingled with ladies of the court, some of whom posed for him, and was elected to the prestigious Pulchri Studio for artists. In winter he indulged in ice skating and made studies of skaters, while summertime excursions to Rotterdam and Amsterdam helped to vary his work. At a sale of the late Dutch King William II's effects at his palace at Tilburg, Johnson purchased a carved oak cabinet that later stood in the dining room of his New York home. Another souvenir of his stay was an antique carved bedstead which he bought in Amsterdam. Before leaving The Hague, Johnson is said to have been offered the enviable position of court painter. If this is true, he declined the post in favor of continuing his education.

Ojibwe Man.
Oil on canvas, 6x11½ inches.

Several of his friends from Düsseldorf had moved on to Paris and Johnson joined them there in August, 1855, taking a studio on the Boulevard Poissoniére. Briefly, he studied with Thomas Couture, a method teacher much in demand with American students, who was working on several commissions for murals. Johnson supposedly copied a head of a sleeping soldier after Couture and was thriving under his tutelage, when he received word of his mother's death. This brought an end to his eclectic European training and Johnson returned home in October.

Johnson was well-equipped to launch himself as a serious painter at this crossroads, but he was somewhat perplexed as to what subjects to paint. There was less demand for portraits now that daguerreotypes had become the rage. At any rate, he had gone to Europe to learn genre painting, not to improve his portrait style. Following his own heart, if also heeding the dictates of this country's artistic community, Johnson was seeking appropriate American themes. While pondering his future, he set off for Superior.

Obviously enchanted with his Indian subjects, Johnson's portfolio depicts a proud people, disinherited, yet possessing an instinctive dignity. If his approach was a romantic one, this was in keeping with his classical training, and also typical of his period. Early nineteenth-century artists commonly idealized American Indians, and even George Catlin was accused by John James Audubon of being "unscientific." To Johnson's credit, he painted individuals, not types, and their images are strikingly realistic. Concerned with producing an accurate historical record, he also detailed their colorful costumes.

Johnson kept these paintings and drawings for himself; they were never exhibited during his lifetime and few people were aware of them. One of these, art critic Henry Tuckerman, a keen advocate of American themes, praised them extravagantly in his *Book of the Artists* of 1867:

In a few years the Indian traits will grow vague; and never yet have they been adequately represented in Art.... A recent glimpse into the portfolio of Eastman Johnson convinced us that he would do peculiar justice to a comparatively unworked mine of native art.... We have never seen the savage melancholy, the resigned stoicism, or the weird age of the American Indian, so truly portrayed: a Roman profile here, a fierce sadness there, a grim withered physiognomy, or a soft but subdued wild beauty, prove how the artist's eye had caught the individuality of the aboriginal face; and with the picturesque costume, to imagine what an effective representative picture of the Red Man of America, with adequate facilities, this artist could execute.

Johnson was working at Grand Portage in the fall of 1857 and may have intended to spend a second winter in the region, but the financial panic that year left him virtually penniless. When property values collapsed in Superior he returned to the East, probably in November, to repair his fortunes. On route, he spent a few months in Cincinnati where a city history relates that despite the fact that he was often "out of pocket," Johnson insisted on the relatively high price of seventy-five dollars for his portraits. Much more like Johnson, says John I.H. Baur, is the story told to him by a nephew of Johnson's who said that one of the portraits his uncle painted, he thought it was in Cincinnati, was for a person who had little money but had a comfortable chair which the artist accepted as payment instead.

Kenne waw be mint.
Charcoal and crayon on paper, 8x7½ inches.
The name means "He Who is Observed."

In the spring of 1858, Johnson had a studio on Washington Square in New York, and was likely at work on his best-known painting, *Life in the South.* Widely praised when it was exhibited at the National Academy of Design in 1859, this ambitious canvas (which depicts contented slaves in their run-down quarters) resulted in Johnson's being elected an Associate of the Academy, starting him on an immensely successful career as a genre painter. Except for a few Indian scenes painted at Murray Bay, Canada, in the summer of 1869, and there were no careful portraits among these, Johnson never painted Indians again. He reportedly returned to Superior in the early 1880s to close up some land transactions, but by then his interests were elsewhere.

Johnson became a full Academician of the National Academy in 1860 and was touted as an artist who could portray the American scene with freshness and honesty. Without being condescending, he painted the homely virtues of country life. One typical picture, *Fiddling His Way,* exhibited in France at the Paris Universal Exposition in 1867, shows a young black man earning his keep by playing his fiddle for a rural family. Johnson's earliest dated rustic painting, *Corn Husking,* was published as a litho-graph by Currier and Ives in 1861. These and his paintings like *Winnowing Grain, The Horse Trade,* and *Bargaining for a Horse,* appealed to mid-century collectors, many of whom were self-made men of humble origins.

During the Civil War years, though he never participated as a soldier, Johnson was present with his paints and pencils at several battles. He wasn't looking for combat scenes but wanted sentimental topics — themes that would be suitable in any parlor. On the back of one painting, *A Ride for Liberty — The Fugitive Slaves,* he wrote: "A veritable incident in the Civil War, seen by myself at Centerville on the morning of McClellan's advance to Manassas. March 2, 1862." At Antietam in September that same year he found the subject for *The Wounded Drummer Boy.* When the finished oil was shown at the National Academy in 1872, the catalogue carried this explanation: "In one of the battles of the late war a drummer boy was disabled by a shot in the leg. As he lay upon the field he called to his comrades, 'Carry me and I'll drum her through.' They tied up his wound, a big soldier took him upon his shoulders, and he drummed through the fight."

Oweenie of the Chippewas.
Oil on canvas, 10½x9½ inches.
This portrait is the only piece in the present collection that was
not part of Richard Teller Crane's gift to the city of Duluth. The
St. Louis County Historical Society purchased it from a
western art dealer in 1983.

Away from the front, Johnson spent the spring months in the early 1860s in the maple sugar camps at Fryeburg, Maine. His temporary studio was a small house built on wheels and equipped with a stove. To his mind, America was at her homespun best amidst the work and merrymaking in the camps, and he made numerous paintings of single figures and groups of people. In addition to picturing workers tapping trees and boiling down the sap in huge kettles to make syrup, he also captured the camps' lighter moments in paintings such as *At the Camp — Spinning Yarns and Whittling, The Story Teller of the Camp,* and *Card Playing at Fryeburg.* These are joyous paintings, proclaiming an American ritual, and Johnson clad his characters in brightly-hued garments to amplify his local color focus.

Another time-honored Johnson painting is his *Boyhood of Lincoln,* executed in the aftermath of the war in tribute to the slain president. Finished in time to hang in the annual exhibition at the National Academy in 1868, this painting's content virtually assured its success. The boy Lincoln is depicted in his log cabin home, intent on a book by the light of the open fireplace. As was sometimes his habit, Johnson made several copies of this painting. (There are also interesting similarities between this painting and the self-portrait of Johnson in his Lake Superior cabin.)

Ojibwe Boy.
Charcoal and crayon on paper, 5x4¾ inches.

In 1869 when he was in his mid-forties, Johnson married Elizabeth Buckley of Troy, New York, and the newlyweds took up residence in the house at 65 West 55th Street in New York that was the artist's home for the rest of his life. The birth of their only child, Ethel, the next year precipitated a series of mother and child paintings by Johnson. Women in general, cast in domestic or decorative roles, appear more frequently in his pictures during this time. The figures are painted more carefully than the backgrounds in these pieces, pointing up once again Johnson's facility as a portraitist, but it would be years yet before he abandoned the genre field.

In the years following his marriage, Johnson became closely associated with Nantucket. He bought property and summered each year with his family on the island, filling canvas after canvas with scenes of the annual cranberry harvest. "The man and the place have a natural sympathy for each other," wrote one critic. "He is a chronicler of a phase of our national life which is fast passing away." Cranberry picking, like maple sugar making, was a uniquely American subject, and one that absorbed Johnson for several years.

Johnson also found willing models for other paintings, many of them interior scenes, among the island's residents. He seems to have been especially fond of retired sea captains. One of these, Captain Charles Myrick, a bewhiskered gentleman in a stovepipe hat, is seen repeatedly in his paintings. Johnson's last dated genre work was *The Nantucket School of Philosophy* (1887) in which a group of elderly men sit reminiscing around a potbellied stove in the local shoemaker's shop. A dozen years later in 1899, the last genre painting he exhibited at the National Academy was *Embers* (painted about 1880). Captain Myrick is the subject of this piece. Seated before an open fireplace, tending dying coals, the bent old man is himself an ember of bygone days.

Studies of Ojibwe Man.
Oil on canvas, 7x12 inches.
Some of Johnson's subjects were undoubtedly half-breeds
rather than full-blooded Indians. This would seem the case with
the man in this study.

During the last twenty years that he painted, beginning about 1880, Johnson gave up genre almost entirely in favor of portraits. Probably he could make a better living from the latter because his fees were substantial: $5,000 for a full-length portrait, $1,500 for a head and shoulders. His clients included John D. Rockefeller, Jay Gould, William H. Vanderbilt, and Presidents Cleveland and Harrison. Commissions came from business organizations, colleges, hospitals, and men's clubs, and it was not unusual for Johnson to work, standing at his easel, from nine or ten in the morning until dark. Portraits that he did of himself, incidentally, including one in which he is dressed in a "Twelfth Night" costume for a party at the Century Club in 1899, were some of his finest.

As he aged, Johnson's usual zest for life waned. He returned to Europe three times in 1885, 1891, and 1897, but except for these respites, continued a rigorous schedule of painting. In a letter from New Bedford dated 1898 to a nephew, he writes: "I have felt so little like work that I have done but little since I left town. It is all up-hill, but I must get at it." From Nantucket, in another letter to the same person, undated but probably written a short time later, he says: "Just a line to tell you we are alive and working miserably every day, fussing, straightening, plastering, mending, puttying, painting, puttying, whitewashing, sodding, just to keep this *shebang* so as *to rent,* or if not, to *live in* when we have no other place. I wish to the Lord I could *sell* it for even *much less* than it has cost me, and that I would never have to come to this island again. I am done with it, but I cannot *throw it* away, and that is what keeps us here now. We are doing our best to get off, and hope to in three days, or it may be four. I am getting very *tired* and *hate* work, would never do another stroke if I could help it...."

Eastman Johnson died at his New York home on April 5, 1906, at the age of eighty-one. He had finished his dinner and gone to his library for a smoke. As he was filling his pipe, he fell dead in his chair. Funeral services were held at St. George's Church, and Johnson's longtime friend, George Hall, was one of his pallbearers.

Canoe of Indians.
Oil on canvas, 17¾x38¾ inches.

Sedong enik.
Oil on canvas, 10x8 inches.
The name means "Very Strong Arm."

Ojibwe Camp Scene.
Oil on canvas, 9½x11½ inches.

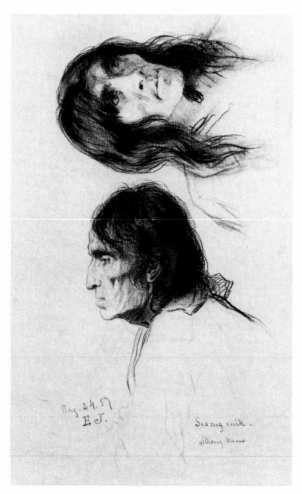

Studies of Ken ne war be mint and Sesong enik.
Charcoal and crayon on paper, 13x7⅞ inches.
The names mean "He Who is Observed" and
"Very Strong Arm."

Midosuay beek.
Charcoal and crayon on paper, 20½x10½ inches.
The name means "Ten Dollars."

Ojibwe Man.
Charcoal and crayon on paper, 6¾x5½ inches.

Hiawatha.
Charcoal and crayon on paper, 15¼x11¼ inches.
This drawing is a preliminary sketch for a pastel painting of the
same subject.

Scene of Wigwam and Family.
Pencil and charcoal on paper, 10½x8 inches. This sketch is on
the back of *Wigemar Wasung.* (page 19).

Indian Grave.
Pencil on paper, 5½x7⅛ inches.
This drawing is on the back of *Ojibwe Man* (page 53).

Notin e garbowik.
Oil on canvas, 12½x9½ inches.
The name means "Standing Wind Woman."

Ojibwe Boy.
Oil on canvas, 7¼x4½ inches.

Kay be sen day way We Win.
Charcoal and crayon on paper, 10¾x14 inches.

Ojibwe Man.
Charcoal and crayon on paper, 7x6½ inches.

Ojibwe Boy.
Charcoal and crayon on paper, 5x4 inches.

Sha men ne gun.
Charcoal and crayon on paper, 21¼x9⅛ inches.

In an effort to clear her husband's studio, Mrs. Johnson authorized an auction of his artwork at the American Art Galleries in New York in February, 1907. The records of this sale indicate that there were once additional paintings in Johnson's Indian collection. Three oils, *Rock-a-Bye-Baby, On a Tree Top,* along with *Grand Portage — Lake Superior,* and *Oweenie of the Chippewas,* all Lake Superior paintings, were among the pieces sold. While *Oweenie of the Chippewas* has been acquired by the St. Louis County Historical Society, the whereabouts of the other two paintings is unknown. A photograph of *Grand Portage — Lake Superior* shows it to be a third view of the Indian encampment, looking south over Lake Superior. Another painting by Johnson called *Minnesota Point,* dated 1856, is owned by a grand-nephew of the artist in St. Paul, Minnesota. Minnesota Point is the long spit of land that separates Lake Superior from the inner harbor of Superior Bay.

If Mrs. Johnson offered the entire Indian collection for the American Art Galleries sale, except for the three paintings sold, it was declined. Later that year she attempted to sell what remained of Johnson's artwork to the Smithsonian Institution. Again the Indian pictures may have been included, but the lot was turned down for lack of funds. Elevator manufacturer Richard Teller Crane saw the Lake Superior collection when it was exhibited at the American Museum of Natural History in New York in February, 1908. He had evidently seen the pictures before, and wrote to the manager of his company's branch office in Duluth:

Some time ago Mrs. Johnson, widow of Mr. Eastman Johnson, showed me, and told me about a lot of pictures she has of Indians which Mr. Johnson painted at Duluth about the years 1855-6.

These pictures are of special interest only to the city of Duluth. As the accuracy and reliability of these pictures can be depended upon as showing the Indians before the city was built, I regard it as of great importance that the city of Duluth should have these pictures.

If the city would like to own these pictures and has any suitable place for them, I should be glad to purchase them and make the city a present of them.

You will please take this matter up with the proper city official.

Members of Duluth's city council voted to accept the offer. On November 20, 1908, the American Museum wrote Mrs. Johnson that the collection was "packed and ready to be shipped west." Once in Duluth, the pictures were housed temporarily in the library room of the Masonic Temple. In addition to the paintings and drawings, Crane's gift included the costume worn by the woman in the *Hiawatha* painting and several other items of Indian apparel which Johnson purchased in the region in the 1850s. In 1929 the collection was turned over to the St. Louis County Historical Society.

Hiawatha.
Pastel on paper, 13½x11 inches.
The title for this piece was probably inspired by Longfellow's
poem, *The Song of Hiawatha*. Johnson posed his subject in
garments he bought for the occasion at Grand Portage.

Ojibwe Women.
Oil on canvas, 19½x20⅛ inches.

Ojibwe Woman.
Oil on canvas, 9½x9¾ inches.

Ojibwe Wigwam at Grand Portage.
Oil on canvas, 10¼x15¼ inches.
Ojibwe wigwams were usually made of birchbark
over a pole frame.

Epilogue

Two years before Eastman Johnson came to the region, the Lake Superior Ojibwe ceded their homelands to the United States government in a treaty signed at La Pointe on Madeline Island in 1854. It was a pivotal event in their history. Assigned to reservations, the Indians were expected to abandon their traditional woodland culture and become self-supporting farmers. To a large extent, this never happened. Instead, while retaining their tribal identity, the Ojibwe have played roles in the area's lumbering, fishing, mining, shipping, and tourism industries.

Known in their own language as Anishinabe meaning "original or first man," their neighbors called them the Ojibwe.*

Historian William Whipple Warren, the son of a white trader and an Ojibwe mother, wrote in the mid-nineteenth century that the name derived from the word o-jib which translates "to pucker." Possibly, he said, it referred to a type of moccasin with a puckered front seam in place of a

tongue which the Indians once wore. He was more inclined to believe, though, that it described the way in which the Ojibwe tortured their prisoners of war — by roasting them until they were "puckered up." More recently, scholar Edmund Jefferson Danziger, Jr., concludes that Ojibwe is a form of o-jib-i-weg meaning "those who make pictographs." For several centuries, Ojibwe priests of the Midéwiwin (Mystic Doings) Society preserved their people's history and knowledge of medicine in symbols on birchbark rolls. These scrolls are perhaps the nearest thing to written records found among Indians north of Mexico.

According to tribal legends the Ojibwe once lived near the great salt ocean, probably at the mouth of the St. Lawrence. By the late sixteenth or early seventeenth century, they began moving west in search of new hunting grounds. The French encountered them at Sault Ste. Marie in 1640, calling them Saulteurs or "People of the Rapids." Later the Ojibwe inhabited both shores of Lake Superior. In the eighteenth century they drove the Dakota from northern Minnesota and took possession of the forfeited forests and prized ricing lakes.

*There are several spellings of the name Ojibwe; common variations are Ojibway and Ojibwa. These people are also called Chippewas, an English corruption of Ojibwe.

The fabled land of Gitche Gumee (as Longfellow called Lake Superior) served the Ojibwe well. Wild game was plentiful and the lakes and streams ran with fish. The Indians clothed themselves in tanned hides and skins and lived in dome-shaped wigwams covered with bark. Using Stone Age tools, they fashioned traps and weapons, wooden bowls, birchbark containers, woven fishnets, musical instruments (drums, rattles, and flutes), snowshoes, sleds, and birchbark canoes.

Ojibwe life was family-centered and tied to the seasons. Each new spring the Indians abandoned their winter hunting camps deep in the woods to celebrate spring in the maple sugar groves. They had no salt and maple sugar was not only a confection, but a seasoning for fish, fruits, vegetables, and cereals as well. In summertime the families gathered on the shore of a good fishing lake near their garden and berry patches. Mostly they planted corn, potatoes, pumpkins, and squash, and picked cranberries, blueberries, gooseberries, and raspberries. The yearly wild rice harvest began in mid-August or early September. While the men poled the canoes, the women took hold of the stalks of rice and knocked the kernels into the boat with a stick. Later in the fall the Indians hunted ducks and fished and trapped or snared small animals such as mink, otter, muskrat, rabbit, and beaver, laying up stores for the coming cold weather.

Life in the winter camps where two or three generations of a family often shared a wigwam was particularly intimate. Each dwelling had its own fire for warmth, but the women usually cooked around a communal fire in the center of the camp. Hunters brought home deer and fox and wolves, and sometimes moose or bear. Young boys were taught the ways of the forest while girls were expected to tend to domestic duties. Evenings were frequently given over to storytelling. At bedtime the family laid its blankets over cedar boughs and rush mats, loosened their clothing, took off their moccasins, and slept with their feet near the fire.

Beginning in the seventeenth century, the fur trade which flourished in the Lake Superior country under French and British regimes did little to alter traditional Ojibwe culture. The Indians became dependent upon white traders for material goods, that much is true, but their semi-nomadic woodland way of living continued relatively unchanged. The Europeans were interested in the Northwest chiefly as a source for furs and did not establish permanent settlements.

Once Americans took control of the area, of course, following the War of 1812, the fabric of Indian life was drastically reshaped. John Jacob Astor's American Fur Company moved into the Ojibwe country, bent on preserving the northland in its wilderness state, and with it the firm's fur profits, but the traders were helpless to turn back the white vanguard fast on their heels. Missionaries, in combination with the federal government, sought to civilize and Christianize the Indians, while miners, lumbermen, and farmers clamored for their lands. It was really only a matter of time, forty years in fact, before the heyday of the fur trader and the Ojibwe trapper was ended, and the Indians were confined to small reservations scattered from Grand Portage to Keweenaw Bay in Michigan.

The 1854 treaty was a first in that the Ojibwe were allowed to remain in their homeland instead of being driven west of the Mississippi. At the same time their reservations were too small to sustain a hunting, fishing, and gathering economy. Until now the Indians had been able to choose those features of civilization which appealed to them. Hereafter they were wards of the Great White Father in Washington. They were thrust headlong down the white man's road, and for nearly a century it led to the disintegration of their culture and left them impoverished.

Until the 1930s the federal government's primary goal on the reservations was to civilize the Indians by eradicating their native traditions and teaching them to till the soil. It was assumed that self-sufficiency and social integration with their white neighbors would follow. Thousands of woodland hunters moved their families to the tracts assigned their bands, and portable birchbark wigwams gave way to one-room log or frame houses.

The problem was that most of the Indians were not interested in farming (which they considered women's work), and those few who tried it had little success. The region's growing season was so short and the climate so cold that even an industrious white farmer could barely eke out a living in the north country. Their old men and women and children might tend small garden patches, but many of the Indian men found work more to their liking in factories in the towns that sprang up on Lake Superior's south shore. Others worked in logging camps or for mining companies, and some signed on as deck hands aboard lake freighters. Meanwhile, white Indian agents were pleased with the rate of acculturation among the Ojibwe. By the turn of the century nearly all of the Indians wore "citizen's dress" and most could speak English.

Despite whatever progress the Bureau of Indian Affairs perceived, however, the Indians were in dire circumstances. Family incomes were low and living conditions on the reservations were usually both substandard and unsanitary. Tuberculosis and alcoholism (the latter a legacy of the fur trade era) became serious health problems. The federal government's prolonged assault on Ojibwe culture had not moved the Indians into the white mainstream as intended, but instead created widespread suffering and discontent on the reservations. Clearly, Washington had blundered in its attempt to Americanize and assimilate its native red men.

During the 1920s countless reformers urged major changes in American Indian policy. They felt that both the government and missionaries had generally failed to study, understand, and take a sympathetic attitude toward Indian ways, Indian ethics, and Indian religion. Surely it would be better to build on what was sound and good in an Indian's own life, they argued. With a national economic depression only worsening the Indians' plight, this line of thinking led to passage of the Indian Reorganization Act in 1934. It was called the Indian New Deal, and for the first time in eighty years the Ojibwe had reason to believe that they might survive as a people.

Importantly, the plan provided for limited Indian self-government on the reservations. It also established a $10 million loan fund to be used for economic development. (Many Ojibwe borrowed money to set themselves up in small farming, fishing, or trapping enterprises.) Recognizing too the insanity of trying to strip the tribesmen of their Indian identity, Congress agreed that henceforth all Native Americans would enjoy "the fullest constitutional liberty, in all matters affecting religion, conscience and culture."

It was a beginning that faltered. Just as the Indians were taking the first meaningful steps toward self-determination, World War II focused the country's attention on defense efforts. Funding for reservation programs was cut and Indian schools, hospitals, agency buildings, vehicles, roads, and telephone networks fell into disrepair. At the war's end, misguided bureaucrats considered the reservations an economic dead end and relocated what tribesmen they could in urban industrial areas. Twenty years later, enervated by poverty, most Ojibwe on their ancestral lands were unemployed, ill-housed, undereducated, and politically submissive.

All this is finally changing. Early in the 1960s the Bureau of Indian Affairs renewed its previous commitment to New Deal policies, and the past two decades have seen a dramatic turnabout in Ojibwe fortunes.

Working through revitalized tribal councils, the Indians themselves are planning and implementing government-supported housing, education, and health programs on the reservations. Federal monies have also launched numerous reservation enterprises, many of them tourist-oriented. The most ambitious of these is a multi-million dollar hotel complex at Grand Portage. (The facility serves visitors to Grand Portage National Monument, an impressive reconstruction that recalls the halcyon days of the North West Company fur post.) Ojibwe leaders are confident that this development is only the first of several that will ultimately permit the phase out of public subsidies. The production of wild rice, some of it cultivated, is another important area industry. Most of the Indians still supplement their diets by hunting, fishing, and picking berries as they have done for hundreds of years, but they are nonetheless firmly footed in the twentieth century.

The Indians take great pride in their Ojibwe heritage. Their strong sense of ethnic identity has been their key to survival. "We are still Indian in spite of a thousand treaties and missionaries with their black frocks," writes Ojibwe author Don Bibeau. "We will endure because we are Indian." Being Indian, he explains, "is not simply living in the forest, or mountains or plains, or skin, features, or beads, or sense of history, or language or song: it is living in peace within the great cycles of nature which the Great Spirit has bestowed upon his children, and it is living within the tribal fold."

Eastman Johnson's Indians were a people dependent upon white men since the prosperous days of the fur trade. With the signing of the 1854 treaty, they were brought to their knees but promised a better tomorrow. That tomorrow may finally be arriving. Three hundred years of domination by outside powers have ended for the Ojibwe. Facing into the wind, but at home in the land of their fathers, the Lake Superior bands are once more charting their own destiny.

Selected Bibliography

Baur, John I. H. *Eastman Johnson, 1824-1906: An American Genre Painter.* Brooklyn: Institute of Arts and Science, 1940. (Reprinted, New York: Arno Press, 1969.)

Danziger, Edmund Jefferson, Jr. *The Chippewas of Lake Superior.* Norman: University of Oklahoma Press, 1978.

Densmore, Frances. *Chippewa Customs.* (U.S. Bureau of American Ethnology, Bulletin 86.) Washington: GPO, 1929. (Reprinted, St. Paul: Minnesota Historical Society Press, 1979.)

French, Edgar, "An American Portrait Painter of Three Historical Epochs." *World's Work* XIII (1906):8307-8323.

Grant, John B., Jr. "An Analysis of the Paintings and Drawings by Eastman Johnson at the St. Louis County Historical Society." Master's thesis, University of Minnesota, 1960.

Heilbron, Bertha L. "A Pioneer Artist on Lake Superior." *Minnesota History* 21 (June, 1940):149-157.

Hills, Patricia. *Eastman Johnson.* New York: Clarkson N. Potter, Inc., 1972.

Walton, William. "Eastman Johnson, Painter." *Scribner's Magazine* XL (1906):263-274.

Warren, William W. "History of the Ojibways, Based Upon Traditions and Oral Statements." *Minnesota Historical Collections* V:23-394 (1885). (Reprinted as *History of the Ojibway Nation.* Minneapolis: Ross & Haines, 1957, 1970.)

Wilson, Mary G. "Five New Works by Eastman Johnson." *The American Art Journal.* Vol. XI, No. 1 (January, 1979):88-90.

In addition to these sources, the author was able to use material in the archives of the St. Louis County Historical Society.

This book was designed by Dale K. Johnston.
The production consultant was Rohland W. Wiltfang.
The typestyle used throughout the book is Univers 55 and 56.
The paper is Warren's lustro dull cream.
This book was printed and bound by
North Central Publishing Inc. in Saint Paul, Minnesota.